THE
ORDINANCE
OF
TITHE
AND THE
NEW TESTAMENT APPROACH

THE
ORDINANCE
OF
TITHE

AND THE
NEW TESTAMENT APPROACH

BISI OLANREWAJU

ARPress
ILLUMINATING IDEAS
EMPOWERING VOICES

ARPress
45 Dan Road Suite 5
Canton MA 02021

Hotline: 1(800) 220-7660
Fax: 1(855) 752-6001

Ordering Information:
Quantity sales. Special discounts are available on quantity purchases by corporations, associations, and others. For details, contact the publisher at the address above.

Printed in the United States of America.

| ISBN-13: | Paperback | 979-8-89389-018-1 |
| | eBook | 979-8-89389-019-8 |

Library of Congress Control Number: 2024908166

DEDICATION

This book is dedicated to all genuine men of God, called into full-time service in the vineyard of God and are committed to their assignment in spite of all odds, especially financially.

CONTENTS

ACKNOWLEDGEMENT

Only the Lord God Almighty who alone gives correct and accurate inspiration must take glory for this book.

Meanwhile, I must say thank you to a few people that God used to encourage the writing of this book. The first is my wife – Felicia Ayodele, who has been on my neck to be doing some teachings on the net, having seen the grace of God upon my life as we interact at home. The next person I must appreciate is Pastor Gabriel Oluwasinmibowale Oyeniyi, who is my prayer partner, when he saw my writings on the facebook, he suggested that I make it a book and that was the encouragement I needed to put this into a book. I also must appreciate my children, they made up the church where I teach some of this things before making it a public materials.

I must also appreciate my nephew, Barrister Femi Matthew Olanrewaju for taken his time to cross the 'ts' and dot the 'is'. God bless you.

There are people I must also acknowledge too, but I do not want to encumber you with names. Everyone that God has been used to bless my family financially are here appreciated. Your sources will never go dry in the mighty name of Jesus Christ.

I must appreciate all the men of God who out of their tight schedules have gone through this book, (Especially Prophet Bolaji Odutayo & Pastor Gbenga Oduniyi and have recommended it to the body of Christ). I must appreciate Pastor Okesola Moses too for his counsel after going through the script. My appreciation goes also to Pastor Abiodun Salako and his amiable wife for their support for this work.

I must not forget my father-in-the-lord, under his ministration in 1989, I gave my life to Jesus Christ. He has been a great blessing to me since then. out of no time he went through the manuscript and made necessary corrections. I pray that God's grace upon your life shall be on the increase in the name of Jesus Christ.

FOREWORD I

A timely written book

This book addresses an issue that is so crucial to the body of Christ, most especially, in our days. This is an issue that has been raised against the Church to the extent that even some that have been steadfast in the will of God have been led astray. And because the issue centres on money, it becomes more sensitive, tempting and a bait in the hand of satan to afflict his victims. His victims? They are, first, the children of God that do not truly understand the mind of God on tithe and as a result neglect it; second, church leaders who for some fears refuse to teach on tithe; third, Church leaders that live flamboyant and extravagant lifestyle from the use of tithe; fourth, the social media self-acclaimed Bible scholars that erroneously condemn the Church for collecting tithes while they also rain abusive words on Pastors, all these among others are the victims of this satan's device. Unfortunately, before the law, ignorance is no excuse.

This book is therefore good for Pastors to study personally, so as to have better and deeper understanding of tithe and also learn how to pass the message to the members of their congregations. It is highly recommended for every child of God to read, even if you are a faithful tither, you need to read this book in order to handle tithing in faith because the word of God says that whatever we do that is not of faith is a sin. So, don't just pay your tithe, pay with knowledge and understanding, so that ignorant men and men of perverse mind will not mislead you with what they call liberated teachings which in actual fact put people of God in bondage.

We live in an age when the earth shall be filled with the knowledge of the glory of the LORD, as the waters cover the sea. However, false knowledge too is on the increase. In order to prevent the Lord's sheep placed under your care from being led astray by strange and contrary doctrine therefore, I will recommend that Pastors should encourage the members of their congregation to read this book. It is self-explanatory. The teaching is simple, straight forward, no twisting of scriptures, yet deep and impactful. This book will bless your soul.

Pastor Gbenga Oduniyi
RCCG Maranatha Parish
Vienna, Austria

FOREWORD 2

Tithe and Tithing has become a major point of discourse lately in the church of God at large. The major reason is because it concerns money and how it is spent. The subject has witnessed a serious attack even amongst brethren in the body of Christ.

A teaching on it is therefore very apt at this point in time.

The barrage of missiles it has received in the recent past may not be unconnected to the warning of Paul the Apostle in his letter to Timothy in 2Timothy 3:1-5. Of particular reference is verse 2 "For men will be lovers of themselves, lovers of money, boasters, proud, blasphemers, disobedient to parents, unthankful, unholy." Satan our adversary has unleashed these on believers in these perilous times hence the arguments for and against God's ordinance which predates the law.

But we bless the name of the Lord for the inspiration He has given Pastor Bisi Olanrewaju to teach on this issue through this small book so that God can speak to us again through this medium to redirect the church on what He had laid down in the scriptures concerning the subject matter.

It is my considered opinion that this book will accomplish the contents of 2Timothy 2:25-26 to correct the heresy that is on-going in the church presently. (25) "in humility (this book is presented in utter humility and in very clear language devoid of ambiguity) correcting those who are in opposition, if God perhaps will grant them repentance so that they may know the truth, (26) and that they may come to their senses and escape the snare of the devil, having been taken captive by him to do his will." The reason is that the new teaching (heresy) had centered on that Christ did not ask for tithe in the New Testament, it is in the law, it is an Old Testament teaching. But this presentation has dealt with these in maximum details.

What is also germane in this book is that it does not force or cajole anyone to pay tithe but the truth of what, how and why are explained therein leaving us in the euphoria of Moses charge to the Israelites in his twilight days when he said to them "This day I call heaven and earth as witnesses against you that I have set before you life and death, blessings and curses. Now choose life so that you and your children may live." Deut. 30:19. (NIV) Would you rather obey God, choose to tithe so that you may receive the abundant blessings and prosperity that you would not have enough space to contain them than to not tithe, deny yourself, rob God and receive the attendant curse? The choice is yours, a la Pastor Bisi.

This book did not only explain why it is expedient to tithe, it also teaches on how the Ministers, Pastors and Leaders of God's congregation should appropriate the tithes as laid down in the scriptures. Pastors should not be feeding fat on the tithes while the have-nots in the church go hungry. It is ordained by God for the purpose of wealth redistribution.

I therefore do not hesitate to recommend this book for teaching in churches, Bible Study Groups, Fellowships as well as those who want to learn more about the what, why and how of tithing for their edification and that of the Body of Christ.

God bless you richly.

Pastor Prophet Bolaji Odutayo
Disciples of Christ Ministry
Lagos.Nigeria.

INTRODUCTION

All glory must go to the Lord Jesus Christ who is the source of our inspiration. This little piece in your hand is as a result of my quest to know the mind of God on tithe for the Church of the New Testament. There is so much noise, arguments and counter arguments on whether or not the members of the body of Christ ought to be paying tithes or not. Many believers are arguing against and some are arguing for. Some leaders of the Lord's people are more confused than their followers. The devil is also playing its own role, usually behind the scene.

There are several challenges in the body of Christ today, a major one out of them is the lack of teachers, and so anybody available is saddled with the teaching responsibility. The Lord made it very clear in His last discussions with the Church that all creatures must be preached to (Mk. 16:15), while the nations are to be taught (Mat. 28:19-20).

Beloved, please read the two scriptures to get the point am making here. Did you notice the difference in those instructions? The creatures: the goat, the hyena, the lion, the dog, the snake, the vulture, just mention it, weren't that what some of us were before we met the Lord, but then after we met the Lord we became joint heirs, we became members of the nation of Christ, citizens of the kingdom of

God and pilgrims of grace – Eph. 2:12-16; Col. 1:13. After conversion to faith, what we need is teaching, the Lord made it very clear that unless they are taught they cannot be baptized. Did you see that? The Master knew that it is only through sound teaching that His body may grow. Preaching to those who are already members of the body of Christ will only stagnate them. It is by teaching them that they can make good spiritual progress. **Beloved, it is not funny to observe that a lot in the body of Christ understood offerings only as the ones collected during fellowships of brethren.** This little piece in your hand is an in-depth teaching on tithes and offerings, am sure the time you spent reading this book will not be a waste.

I have found grace to make this contribution to this age long doctrine of the Church and I may never take the glory for it. It is therefore written in simple language that anyone may read and comprehend. May the Holy Ghost keep you company as you go through this.

I want to plead with everyone who is reading this little book to be ready to swallow some bitter pills, but I can assure you that it will bless you and your ministry. Teachings inside this book are based on the inspirations I received coupled with personal observations in the body of Christ. There are parts of it that you will read and it will look like it is your story that is being told here, you don't need to feel bad about that. I see that as God being mindful of you. He only wants things to get better for you. Beloved, this is not a book aimed at judgment, no; the aim is to correct, encourage and counsel – 2 Tim. 3:16-17. It is therefore with trembling that I present this to the body of Christ. May it bless you in the mighty name of Jesus Christ.

I will be glad if you can prayerfully and diligently go through this book for proper digestion and assimilation. It will also gladden my heart and I know that God will also be delighted if after you have gone through it, you can recommend to others. Remain blessed.

Above all my desire in the long run is that God will be glorify and His people blessed.

CHAPTER 1

Tithe was Ordained Before the Law

God bless you friends. It is a pleasure to, along with you, examine God's word on the subject of tithes, a subject that has recently brought about intense debates amongst the body of Christ.

I would begin by examining what a tithe is: Tithe ordinarily means a tenth of your earning, or incomes, or profits or even gifts

Meanwhile, this is what the Lord Jesus Christ said on tithe -

> *"Woe to you, teachers of the law and Pharisees, you hypocrites! You give a tenth of your spices--mint, dill and cumin. But you have neglected the more important matters of the law--justice, mercy and faithfulness. You should have practiced the latter, without neglecting the former.* (NIV)

> *"What sorrow awaits you teachers of religious law and you Pharisees. Hypocrites! For you are careful to tithe even the tiniest income from your herb gardens, but you ignore the more important aspects*

of the law—justice, mercy, and faith. You should tithe, yes, but do not neglect the more important things. (NLT)

First, I like to say that faithful tithers in the Church are obedient believers, and by this I do not mean that all faithful tithers are believers. Faithful tithers are helping God to pay His bills and that makes God their covenant partners in whatever they are involved with. They also, through their obedience, create a divine hedge around their wealth and health. As we go into the discussions on this phenomenon in the Church today, you will get better understanding on several issues.

Many are raising objections on this subject for different reasons. For some, it is ignorance. Some are deliberately raising their voices against it because they do not like the way it is being used. There are others who are raising their voices against it because they feel that it is enriching the leaders of the churches. There are yet others who are raising their voices against it because they are rich and when they look at what is going to tithing or what should be going into it, it is much and they assume that everyone is paying it, so they are looking for other members of the church to support their position in case they stop paying, so that they may not be seen as being disobedient to the law of God. They feel that if it is a corporate agreement, God may not be angry with them. They do not understand that tithe is not a law issue; especially considering that the body of Christ as it is today is not even under the law!

I must let you know friends, that tithing is not a matter of the law. God deliberately instituted this before giving the law. The first man that paid tithe was Abram (Abraham), whom we all accept as the father of faith – Gen. 14:18-20. So, it is not an ordinance to the Israelites alone. Tithing began before there was a nation called Israel. Abram met Melchizedek, who in my own understanding was Jesus Christ, because the scripture testified that he was

> *"Without father, without mother, without descent, having neither beginning of days, nor end of life; but made like unto the Son of God; abideth a priest continually."* Heb. 7:3.

Only Jesus Christ perfectly fits into this description. The truth of the matter then is that the Lord Jesus Christ had visited the earth several times before He came in the person of Jesus of Nazareth (Gen. 19:20-21; Dan. 3:25). It was during one of such visitations that Abram met Him when he was returning from the slaughter of the kings – Heb. 7:1. Technically therefore, it means that the first person who collected tithe was Jesus Christ. Though as the Jesus of Nazareth he never collected tithe from anybody (at least it was not on record that He collected any). All that He collected was offerings at different fora – Mat. 14:15-18; Mat. 15:32-38; Mat. 21:1-7; Luk. 5:1-3 (we shall discuss this in rich details in another chapter).

When He gave the law to Moses, God made it very clear why they must pay tithes and He outlined what it must be used for. With the advent of the law, the service of the tabernacle was instituted and there were people saddled with the responsibilities of carrying out the duties in the tabernacle and these people were to do nothing other than the works in the tabernacle and on the altar. God ordered that these people must do nothing else, so that they might be able to concentrate on the assignment in the tabernacle. The Yoruba people in their wisdom said, if you will not allow me to work, then you must supply my needs. This exactly is what the Lord decided to do with His people by adding tithe to the requirements of the law. God made it part of the law so nobody would have the excuse not to pay it. You know, the law has a way of forcing people to do what they ought to do. Beloved, I am sure you know that, but for the law, so many citizens will not pay their taxes. In fact with the enactment of the law that makes the payment of taxes mandatory in nations, many still do all that is possible to evade taxes, and that is bad.

The payment of tithes under the law was mandatory, but there seemed to be no punishment for evaders as it was when other laws were broken. This is however dangerous, because it means that God will handle it by Himself. I believe that it was so because it might be difficult for a fellow man to be able to measure the blessing God has given to their fellows. It is only God who knows what He has done for individuals. That is why God calls it robbery when you are not paying tithe. It is not just stealing. Stealing is done most of the time behind the owner or under cover, but robbery is done while the owner is wide awake. It is the reason robberies are done most of the times with arms. Another reason there seemed to be no punishment proscribed for tithe evaders under the law is that those who were to execute the laws were the beneficiaries of the same tithes from the people and they possibly would not be good judges over a matter that directly involved them. Consider this: when the law makers were asked to review their emoluments/salaries, they did so in their own favour. This may be a reason many Pastors do not emphasize or teach deeply about tithes in their assemblies but the truth of the matter is, both the Pastors and the members are losing. I read about a man of God who pastored an assembly of the people of God for ten years and never took offerings. According to that story, what he suffered pastoring there has no second class. The people he pastored also remained poor. He later returned there to apologize to them for that error after he got understanding about this. My counsel is that leaders who understand these things should teach their members through the leading of the Holy Spirit not minding what the people will say, even if it's one person that will understand and follow such teachings, you would have done your own part. There are members of the body of Christ who would have done better if they knew the truth. However such teachings must not be motivated by the flesh. I can remember back then as a child in the Church, no deep teaching on several doctrines of the Bible and tithe wasn't an exception. In fact, to show that neither the leaders nor the congregants understood what tithe was, some would have paid their tithes to December in June, because the tithe book was brought out periodically and read to the whole Church and you know what, we just laughed over it, no one felt that anything was wrong with that practice, it wasn't that the people cannot understand, it was that no one understood what was right, so how could they have taught it. This must not continue if we must experience real wealth in the Church.

So what did God do to encourage the payment of tithes? He added incentives for obedient tithers.

> *"Bring ye all the tithes into the storehouse, that there may be meat in mine house, and prove me now herewith, saith the LORD of hosts, if I will not open you the windows of heaven, and pour you out a blessing, that there shall not be room enough to receive it."* Mal. 3:10

CHAPTER 2

The Ordinance of Tithe in the Law

We have tried to define what tithe is in the last chapter. It will help further to touch on it here again; tithe is the tenth part of your income, earning or profits on your business engagements and gifts.

> *"And concerning the tithe of the herd, or of the flock, even of whatsoever passeth under the rod, the tenth shall be holy unto the LORD."* (Lev. 27:32 KJV)

At different points God through Moses, spoke to the Israelites on tithe and since Israel is a type of the Church, we have a lot to learn from their journeys and life encounters. You know that

Stephen, full of the Holy Ghost in his defence in the Acts of Apostles even referred to them as the church in the wilderness – Acts 7:38. And in the book of first Corinthians chapter ten in verse eleven, Apostle Paul informed the Church of Christ that all the things that happened to them were recorded for us as examples, so that we may learn through them and that we may not falter where they did.

We must know that the Christian faith is a way of life based on given instructions. The Israel race was chosen to help us understand the ways God wants to be dealing with His own people, those who will agree to follow Him. They were not to be asking questions and challenging His authorities over any instruction given to them, obedience is the key (Lev. 18:5; Deut. 28:1; Isa. 1:19). It is the same with Christianity, man has missed it way back in the Garden of Eden. In that singular event that happened in the Garden of Eden, man lost everything to Satan and he has imparted his sinful nature into man. Therefore, man also like him, began to question the authority of God. Whenever God gives man instruction, man always wants to know why. And so when man cannot understand particular instructions given by God, he refuses to follow it to his own peril. This is the reason God sent His Son, first to show us how God wanted to be worshiped (in spirit and in truth) and then to open for us the way back to our Maker.

God has seen the present status of the Church from the beginning, which is the reason He ordained tithe before the law. He knows that this time will come when knowledge would have increased and men will become so crafty to find a way of dodging His instructions. If you consider the first Man who received tithe, with the description the scripture gave Him, He possibly did not need the tithe He received from Abram. He is all sufficient. Offering is what He actually would have preferred to take from man, which was the reason the giving and receiving of offering preceded the ordinance of tithe – Gen. 4:3-4. But God understands the nature man had received from Satan, so He had to help man by receiving tithe from him. You possibly will notice that it was only once that it was recorded that Abraham paid tithe, but God continuously took offerings from him – Gen. 12:8; 13:4; 18; 15:9; 18:1-8; 22:1-2. These are the ones recorded in the scriptures. I believe there were other times that He made offerings to the Lord, which were not recorded.

Why did God ordain tithe?

So the question then is why did God ordain tithe? I have explained a bit of this in the last chapter, but we shall go a bit deeper here, because there are scriptures that many in the church have come across that they seem not to understand and they are erroneously teaching same in the body of Christ out of context. The Lord Jesus Christ referred to them as the blinds leading the blind – Mat. 15:14. There is no better time than now to correct such erroneous teachings. I pray that God may give us the understanding required for this. I have said it before somewhere, revelation is what a man requires to move in the direction God desires that he should go.

Tithe was instituted among the people of God for several reasons, which include (but are not limited to): Catering for His under-shepherds, leaders of His people and those who may be working on the altar with them. The second is for wealth redistribution among His people. So let's see the scripture where these were stated clearly.

> *"And all the tithe of the land, whether of the seed of the land, or of the fruit of the tree, is the LORD'S: it is holy unto the LORD.* (Lev. 27:30)
>
> *Thou shalt truly tithe all the increase of thy seed, that the field bringeth forth year by year."* (Deut. 14:22)

Two things are clearly stated in these two scriptures: tithes belong to the Lord and it is holy. Since it is holy, it becomes an accursed thing when it remains in your hands – Jos. 7. (Please friends take your time to read this scripture it may be the reason you are facing what you are facing in your businesses). God also expects that all your increase must be tithed. That is why He frowns at those whose income or profits increased and they refuse to increase their tithes. He can remove the increase that He has given you and nobody can do anything about it. He could raise anybody against you, even your most loyal person to achieve this.

> *"Thus speak unto the Levites, and say unto them, When ye take of the children of Israel the tithes which I have given you from them for your inheritance, then ye shall offer up an heave offering of it for the LORD, even a tenth part of the tithe."*
> Num. 18:26

> *"Bring ye all the tithes into the storehouse, that there may be meat in mine house, and prove me now herewith, saith the LORD of hosts, if I will not open you the windows of heaven, and pour you out a blessing, that there shall not be room enough to receive it."* Mal. 3: 10

These two scriptures are explicit on the major reason God ordained tithe. It is that those working on the altar may have food to eat. This is the reason it may be wrong for you to be complaining that your leader is eating your tithe. God said it is their inheritance. They are to give offering out of it and you are not the one to tell them who they may give the offering to. It is God that must instruct them and not you. Tithes are not for Church projects unless the leader decides to use it for projects and when they do so to the neglect of the people working with them on the altar, they have God to answer.

> *"At the end of three years thou shalt bring forth all the tithe of thine increase the same year, and shalt lay it up within thy gates: And the Levite, (because he hath no part nor inheritance with thee,) and the stranger, and the fatherless, and the widow, which are within thy gates, shall come, and shall eat and be satisfied; that the LORD thy God may bless thee in all the work of thine hand which thou doest."*
> (Deut. 14:28-29)

The scripture quoted above is the most misunderstood of all scriptures about tithing. It is better to start reading from verse 22 actually, but I have selected these two verses because of the way I have seen people quoting and explaining them. This scripture is simply telling the Church that tithing is a way of redistributing that which the Lord may have committed to the hands of some members of the Church. The onus is on the leaders to make sure that they are fair in doing this. The scripture says that this must be done at three years intervals, but I think it should not be restricted to a once in three years event. Yes, during the time it was ordained, it may be possible since the counting of their national year began with the exit from Egypt, but in our time, my three years at work may not be my brother's three years and your three years in the kingdom is most likely not my own three years. So it may be proper to allow the

Church to handle this as appropriate. There is so much that may be done through this blessings that God is giving the Church, especially where the collection is much. Scholarship may be given to children that are brilliant but have no means of paying school fees, some may be trained in different trades, empowerment programmes may be done and those who exemplified themselves in such empowerment training may be aided to take-off and monitored, widows and orphans in the church should be catered for from the tithes the church collects. God does not want the leaders to be living in luxury while several members of the body of Christ you are leading are suffering. I believe this is the reason the Lord added this to the ordinance of tithe in the law.

You can see then that God is mindful of everybody in the body of Christ. He knows that it is not everyone in the Church that will be financially buoyant as to need no support from others, but then He wants those who are wealthy amongst His people to pick the bill of others on His behalf. You may now see the reason He added the incentives with the ordinance of tithe.

> *"Bring ye all the tithes into the storehouse, that there may be meat in mine house, and prove me now herewith, saith the LORD of hosts, if I will not open you the windows of heaven, and pour you out a blessing, that there shall not be room enough to receive it."* Mal. 3:10.

What you must know is that Satan is not comfortable with the blessing of the Lord's people. He would have loved a situation where everybody in the Church is poor. When everybody in the Church of Christ is poor, it will be a way to discourage the people from following the Lord and He knows that disobedience to this instruction will send wealthy people in the Church back to poverty. He will stop at nothing to discourage it. God wants His people liberated and that is why you are reading this. If you know anybody in the body of Christ who was very wealthy before and went back to poverty, please check, this may be the reason. Evasion of tithe and offering is a sure way back to poverty. Beloved watch! Satan is a dangerous adversary, but he has lost the battle over your life already.

CHAPTER 3

Why Tithe and Offering?

In the Garden of Eden we were not told that Adam and the woman offered anything to God. This was because, there was no need for such. In the Garden of Eden, where they lived, all they needed were supplied without sweat. The presence of evil was not there. The works of their hand were blessed unhindered. They put in little effort to get much. There was nothing they needed to do to sweat, all things answered to their beck and call. They were living in the presence of the LORD. In the Garden of Eden, they were innocent beings, they knew nothing like good or evil, so they were not capable of doing either –Gen. 2:17. There was no shortage of anything that they needed, everything they needed they got at the snap of their fingers.

They needed no rain to grow their crops, water came up from the ground to water their garden – Gen. 2:5-6. In that Garden, there was no weed, no thistle, unwanted plants don't grow on their farms, and everything was perfect. God never gave them the ordinance of tithe or offering. What for? No one needed it there, it was the reason I said earlier that the One who received the first tithe does not need it really. God ordained it for our generation, but He must institute it with the father of faith. So that everyone who will come under the covenant of Abraham may be able to identify with it.

Let's consider the reason God ordained tithe and offering again:

> *"Will a man rob God? Yet ye have robbed me. But ye say, Wherein have we robbed thee? In tithes and offerings. Ye are cursed with a curse: for ye have robbed me, even this whole nation. Bring ye all the tithes into the storehouse, that there may be meat in mine house, and prove me now herewith, saith the LORD of hosts, if I will not open you the windows of heaven, and pour you out a blessing, that there shall not be room enough to receive it. And I will rebuke the devourer for your sakes, and he shall not destroy the fruits of your ground; neither shall your vine cast her fruit before the time in the field, saith the LORD of hosts. And all nations shall call you blessed: for ye shall be a delightsome land, saith the LORD of hosts."* Mal. 3: 8-12

If you diligently study this scripture, you will notice that every reason behind this ordinance called tithe and offering is to the benefit of man. God does not eat food, it is those working in His house that He planned to make the food available to. And the one who faithfully gives his tithe and offering is also benefiting, because God promised to keep your blessings on the increase and to give a covering to the blessings.

Offering was ordained so we may show our gratitude to God who does not allow the seed we sowed to be a waste and also gives increase to it.

The fact that a man may sow and labour and have nothing to show for all his commitment is to let you know how heavily Satan has dealt with the children of men. Satan's desire is to make you go out and return without finding pasture. And in the event that you find pasture, he does not want you to enjoy what you have laboured for and that is the reason God instituted that which will give you an edge over his antics. Satan noticed that by the incursion he made on God's plan for man in the Garden of Eden, God placed a curse over man because he went in the way of the counsel of Satan, but Satan could notice God's mercy in that curse, God said you may have to sweat to have food on your table but the fact that you will have food on your table showed that God is still mercifully mindful of you (Gen. 3:17-19), and your arch enemy is not comfortable with that, it is the reason Satan will always come around to see what you are doing. When he sees that a man is making progress, especially those who belonged to God, he is not happy, so he wants to do everything possible to spoil your joy. He wants to frustrate your efforts, he wants to proof that he is the prince of this place (Jhn. 14:30), but those who are running under the new covenant through the blood of the lamb and are faithful in their tithe and offering have a hedge around their possession. You remember what he said about Job?

> *"... Doth Job fear God for nought? Hast not thou made an hedge about him, and about his house, and about all that he hath on every side? thou hast blessed the work of his hands, and his substance is increased in the land."* Job. 1:9-10.

This showed that the devil will always come around those who are of the Lord with the intention to kill, to steal, and to destroy – Jhn. 10:10a. When it is those who belonged to him, he doesn't really have problem with them, he knows that as far as those ones are concerned, they belonged to him and he could do anything with them any time. So the scripture said - ***Fret not thyself because of evildoers, neither be thou envious against the workers of iniquity. For they shall soon be cut down like the grass, and wither as the green herb."*** Psa. 37:1-2.

The devil has nothing good for his loyalists (sinners and wicked people); his intention for them is destruction. It is the reason you must not compare yourself with an unbeliever, your destinations are different, hence you cannot afford to board the same vehicle. You must therefore do everything within your capacity never to listen to anyone telling you not to respect the ordinance of tithe and offering, because such individuals are agents of the devil and their intention is to place you in the hand of the devil, their master.

There are many in the church, faithful individuals, who are doing their best to please the Lord and they are wondering why they haven't gotten their breakthroughs, they seemed to be crawling. Meanwhile their colleagues who are compromising standards and are not bothered about the mind of God concerning all they are doing, are making it and living in luxury. If it stopped at that it may be okay, but this ungodly people are smearing it at the face of these righteous ones, mocking them and their God. So they are asking questions; why is God tolerating these evil doers? Sometimes you desire that God's judgment will come immediately. May I let you know that you are not alone in this experience, Job also was bothered like you which is the reason he said –

"Wherefore do the wicked live, become old, yea, are mighty in power? Their seed is established in their sight with them, and their offspring before their eyes. Their houses are safe from fear, neither is the rod of God upon them. Their bull gendereth, and faileth not; their cow calveth, and casteth not her calf. They send forth their little ones like a flock, and their children dance. They take the timbrel and harp, and rejoice at the sound of the organ. They spend their days in wealth, and in a moment go down to the grave." Job. 21:7-13

(you may please read the whole chapter). But It didn't take too long for Job to understand the mind of God concerning such people – *"Have ye not asked them that go by the way? and do ye not know their tokens, That the wicked is reserved to the day of destruction? they shall be brought forth to the day of wrath."* (Job 21:30)

This is the reason you must not consider their ways, never contemplate to walk in their counsel, nor stand in their ways, nor seat in their seat – Psa. 1:1-3.

Beloved, watch and pray is the counsel of the Master as He was approaching the end of His ministry on the earth – Mat. 13:33. Satan is doing all that is within his capacity to make sure that those who understand the secret behind God's intention for instituting tithes and offerings and have keyed into it are discouraged from observing it. His desire is to use your own hands to remove the covering that is over that which the Lord has given you. This place is given to Satan and his allies for now. Tithe and offerings are God's way of pushing back the hands of the evil from your businesses and concerns. Can you please take a few minutes to pray this simple prayer – Father in the name of Jesus Christ, I stand against any plan of the devil to pitch me against God and against my progress in life . Every power working against my understanding about this ordinance is scattered in the name of Jesus Christ

The real reason God gave the wisdom to tithe and to do offering is to restrict Satan from tampering with His own people and everything that belonged to them. You must know this beloved, that paying of tithe, being generous with your offering does not guarantee you a place in heaven. The same way not observing this ordinances cannot be a hindrance to your getting home safely. However, another chapter will let you know what real dangers awaits those who evades tithe. Keeping Satan away from you and that which is yours is just a tip of the ice-barge.

CHAPTER 4

Offerings Were First Ordained and they are Better than Tithes

The ordinance of offerings began before tithes and it was better than tithes. It began with the fruits (offspring) of the first family. Their names were Cain and Abel – Gen. 4:3-5. These guys were born after the curse on man and so whatever they were doing becomes subject to satanic influences and manipulations. So, they understood this and they also knew that if not that God was on their side, their efforts on their businesses would have been wasted. So when they had those harvests they thought it wise to give back to God who gave them the increase.

Three things principally, were the reasons they began to give offering to God; to show their appreciation to the One who gave them the increase, to provoke further increase and to show that they belonged to the Father of light from whom all good things come – Jam. 1:17. Two principal factors determines the acceptability of offerings; the giver and the quality of the offering given. By the giver, I mean the personality of the giver and the motive behind the giving. By quality,

I mean the value of the offering to the giver and the source of the offering.

Offerings are supposed to be done voluntarily, you will notice that the first persons that came to God with their offerings were not commanded so to do. They just knew by instinct that it is the right thing to do. We were not informed that their parents gave offerings to the Lord at any given time. So it looked like they were not taught. God expects that all of His children will know that this is the right thing to do, especially by the leading of the Holy Spirit that is inside you. Giving of offering is an indication that you understand that all things belonged to God and that it is a special privilege that these things are in your possession. You must have noticed that it is not all who were engaged in what you are engaged in that are making it. So, you just pause to ask the question, why me? Unfortunately, it is those who feel they are not doing well in what they are involved with that asks this question most of the time. Many who are doing well in their businesses and so has become wealthy even in the Church are of the opinion that it is because they knew how to do things right that they are making it, many of them think that those who are not doing well in their professions, trades or businesses are lazy, they think they are not wise or smart enough. That may not be correct. May I please plead with you to stop thinking so? A man who thinks this way will not be a blessing to the people around him as he ought to be and he may even find it difficult to give back to God. I know a man who does not know how to do simple additions of money back then in my village, if you go to him to buy things, all you need do to cheat him was to pay him with notes of lesser denominations of money, so he may have plenty notes to count, after he would have counted the money over and again, he will tell the customer that it is complete, meanwhile he has been shortchanged, in fact people call him *'owo e m'ago'* (*'money miss road'*), but his wealth was increasing. How do you explain that? It is God that really gives men power to get wealth – Deut. 8:18. This you must box into your system dear rich man that it is not by power nor by might, as the Lord enlarges your coast – Zec. 4:6.

So friends, you must not be coerced or cajoled to give offerings, this is one factor that determines the quality of what you are offering. When you understand that all that you are belonged to the Lord I think it becomes easier to offer to Him all that you have. Only children are pampered, lured, cajoled or even forced to do what they are required to do. When a believer is not faithful in tithe and offering, it is an indication that he/she is not matured.

The first tithe was also done voluntarily, Abraham, on his way back from the slaughter of the kings, met Melchizedek king of Salem and gave him the tithe of all without the receiver asking for it (Heb. 7:1-2), it was accepted and blessed. But we saw that under the Law of Moses it became a must and in fact according to the record in Malachi, curse was placed on any one who evades tithe – Mal. 3:8-9, because it is like trying to discredit the faithfulness of God. The Lord Jesus Christ made it very clear, teaching and answering questions from the Pharisees in Matthew chapter nineteen that the law was added as a result of the hardness of the people's heart – Mat. 19:8. Under the same Moses, God instructed His people to build Him a temple. You will notice that God did not ask Moses to build the temple from the tithes of the people, rather, He asked him to go to the people to explain what He has instructed him to do and then take offerings from only those who had willing hearts – Exo. 25:1, here is a lesson for us all ministers on the altar and the laity, God does not want us to do anything for Him if it is not from a willing heart. This is the reason I said offering is preferred to tithe. In another chapter, we shall see how and why the Lord Jesus Christ only received offerings as He went about His earthly ministry. God does not receive an offering that does not have the qualities He desired and we have said what these qualities are; the value the offering has to you, the source of it and who you are. It's good to let you know that it is not all the offerings that people seemed to give to Him (God) that He receives.

Another thing that should be a matter of concern to all the children of God is that all the offerings that Moses received on behalf of God were commanded. It then means that beyond giving to God voluntarily, is the question; does God need the offering you are giving? Is He the One commanding you to give the offering? And to the man of God too who may be reading this, who is commanding you to receive offering from the people? I know you want to build a cathedral, a larger tent, because the congregation is increasing every day. Is that enough reason to build a bigger one? It make sense so to do, but our senses are not enough to do God's work sir/ma. You may be doing things that makes sense without the One who sent you commanding it. Was it not a good thing that David wanted to build a place of rest for the ark of the Lord's oracles? But the owner of the ark said;

'No, I have not ordained you to build me an ark.'

And that settled it – 1 Sam. 7:1-5; Chro. 17:1-4. It is not all that made sense to a man that God ordained. Sir/Ma, it is not enough to gather your followers and seek their opinion or counsel on issues that pertained to the kingdom matters, God must have the only say. That was exactly what David did (calling Nathan), it is not the correct thing to do. It is the owner of the work that must dictate what must be done. It is after the Lord has spoken that you may now call your followers to inform them of what the Lord has commanded you to do and that is not also subject to their approval. Moses never sought the approval of his followers to execute the project God gave him, and because it was the LORD who sent Him, he got all the supports he needed. Today, many leaders in God's vineyard will have to get approval on a project that God laid on their hearts to do from their followers because they believed that it is those people that will fund the project. This is the reason many projects that God actually gave to His servants are failing. He gave the vision of what to do but He was not given the funding and the oversight of the project and so He stood aloof.

God knows what to do when He commanded a work to be done for Him, offering is the way to handle it. Tithes may not be used to fund God's projects, it may not be enough to do it. He also does not want the priests, whose the tithes are to suffer. That is why you should not consider the number of your followers to kick start any work for the Lord. Keep your focus on the One who called you, faithful and just is He. God can send anybody to you from anywhere to fund His project. He's got the whole world in His hands. It may surprise you to know that God can take offering from anybody, Christians and non-Christians. Peter wasn't a disciple when the Lord used his boat remember – Lk. 5:1-10. The reason many members of the body of Christ are misbehaving is that they feel that without them, God's work may not be done, because they noticed that the eyes of the leader is on them whenever there is a project on ground. This must stop, else God can always get an alternative to get His work done. I have seen God do this many times over. Moses felt he was the champion, with all the Lord has done through him. When God saw that he was becoming bigger than his jacket, God changed him. May God not change you. Beloved, God wants a voluntary-cheerful giver. In rebuilding the Jerusalem walls, the scripture confirmed that the nobles of the land did not put their hands to the work – Neh. 3:5, yet God accomplished His purpose with the seemingly feeble hands – Ezr. 6:15; Neh. 6:15. Hello dear Pastor/leader, you need not panic because the nobles are not supporting the course of God in your hands, trust the Lord and the work will prosper. In fact sometimes the reason God allowed the nobles to falter is because God wants to know who you are depending on and He also uses it as an avenue to raise other people that He may depend on.

It is obvious that offerings were ordained long before the institution of tithes or even the law, however through the pages of the Bible offerings were commanded for the work of God and obviously more dependable than tithes. The work of God cannot be limited to tithes, hence, not much will be achieved. Sometimes the tithes that may be collected from 1000 people may not be compared in volume to the offerings that two people will give, since tithe is defined as tenth part of one's earnings, it has place a barricade on what may be paid. There are therefore different kinds of offerings commanded by the Lord that His people may give: burnt offerings (Gen. 22:2; Exo. 29:18), First fruit offerings (Deut. 18:4), wave offerings (Exo. 29:24), sin offerings (Exo. 29:14), meat offerings (Exo. 29:41), thanksgiving offerings (Lev. 7:12), etc. Please note that when God commands, He still respects your will and so your willingness is still required, after all the scripture says that willingness determines acceptance – 2 Cor. 8:12

Let me end this chapter by saying that offerings are higher levels of giving than tithes, only mature Christians gets there. When your commitments to God's work is limited to tithes and offering times in your local assembly, you are not a mature Christian. Can you imagine that one of the reasons God made sure that Cornelius heard the gospel was his acts of giving - Acts 10.

CHAPTER 5

Tithe and Offering in the Early Church

In the Church that Peter and his colleagues presided over – which is normally referred to as the early Church, tithe wasn't a recurrent decimal. The reasons they did not collect tithe from their followers were obvious. The first was that their Master never collected tithe from anybody, though He made it very clear that tithe ought to be paid –Mat. 23:23, and the second was the reason for the first; just like their Master, they were not the authorities in charge of the synagogue. The priests were the ones that presided over the existing system, so there was no way they could tell the people to be bringing their tithes. Already they had issues with that existing system, because the priest were instrumental to the crucifixion of the Lord Jesus Christ. Meanwhile these Apostles were going about proclaiming his resurrection and that it was only by believing on Him that forgiveness of sin and salvation may be granted to anyone. And that was an offence to that existing system. If they now have to be taking tithes from the congregants who were coming to faith through the testimonies they were sharing about their Master, they will be biting more than they can chew.

But as soon as the number of people believing in their messages increased, there also arose the need to cater for them. Some of the people gathering with them had daily needs that must be met (Acts 6:1). Good enough there were also people who gathered with them that had more than enough to share. So what those who had did was to bring what they had to the Apostles for onward distribution to those who may need them. I have said earlier on that tithes and offerings are God's chosen way of redistributing the wealth amongst His people. He already told His people that there will always be the poor amongst them and they must be catered for.

> *"For the poor shall never cease out of the land: therefore I command thee, saying, Thou shalt open thine hand wide unto thy brother, to thy poor, and to thy needy, in thy land."* – Deut. 15:11.

However, I think God does not want anyone in His body to remain poor till thy kingdom come. The poor in the Church this year should not remain the poor after a few years, the status must change - Amen. The one who is benefiting from the benevolence of the others today should, in a not too far distant future become a blessings to others too. The Church should look for every means possible to empower the members of the body, because more people are coming. The duties of the Church should not just be to prepare people for heaven; while those heaven bound people are still in the body, they need that which will make their bodies to be in the good shape that may be able to carry the Master about correctly. Heaven bound people also need food and shelter.

In the early Church, they owned all things in common:

"And all that believed were together, and had all things common; And sold their possessions and goods, and parted them to all men, as every man had need. And they, continuing daily with one accord in the temple, and breaking bread from house to house, did eat their meat with gladness and singleness of heart, Praising God, and having favour with all the people. And the Lord added to the church daily such as should be saved." Acts 2:44-47

The fact that they owned all things common was one of the reasons the Church increased daily. People will normally go to where their needs are met. Is it possible to do the same today? If the man of God over your assembly suggests this today, what would be your response? What they were practicing was something the economist of today will call true communism. But you know what, the devil has crept into the Church. It is difficult to get such followers now, just as much as it is difficult to get the kind of leadership the Apostles in the early Church also provided. The Apostles weren't looking for personal properties to acquire, the followers were not thinking of personal estates, as it was difficult to identify the Master amongst them, so it was difficult to know who the leaders were amongst them, at least not with dressing or the kind of houses they were living in or the kind of food they were eating. What distinguished them was the anointing. There are men of God in our days who will host programmes and they will never eat the kind of food they give to the congregants. We know you have been labouring in prayers and in fasting, that is not a justification for such selfish attitude. You placed yourself in a class you do not belong, your followers are wondering and asking questions. Pride is already setting in and you do not seem to see it sir/ma. There are yet other Pastors when they are invited to minister, you will be surprised at their demands to be able to honour such invitation. You cannot but wonder if it is the same message the likes of Apostle Paul preached they are coming to deliver. This is the time to change, the Master could come any time, am sure you know this truth. Sir/Madam, do not just whisk away this message, please take your time to pray about this and hear what the Holy Ghost may whisper to you, because this was not what the early Church did. The Lord Jesus Christ according to the records available to us never said that He was specially treated anywhere He went with His disciples. In all the places He was invited to what was given to Him to eat was what His followers ate. So, who gave us this template we are working with? There are Pastors who are the sole signatory to the account of their assembly, and that wasn't because they don't have trusted people; some others have their spouses as the finance secretary and the treasurer at the same time. Some others, it is either their brothers, cousins or nephews. The issue of overseeing the account came up in the early Church and the Apostles' suggestion was

> *"… brethren, look ye out among you seven men of honest report, full of the Holy Ghost and wisdom, whom we may appoint over this business. But we will give ourselves continually to prayer, and to the ministry of the word."* (Acts 6:3-4)

They could have suggested their relatives to do the job, but no, they didn't do that. They considered the ministry of the word and prayer to be more demanding than to add that of accounting procedure with it, but what do we hear in the Church today? *'These members are not trustworthy, you can't commit such sensitive matter to their hands',* after they have followed you for more than two years, the simple truth is that you (yourself) are not trustworthy because you are the one who trained them. How long do you think Apostle Paul, during his missionary journeys, spent with his converts before committing those assemblies to their hands? Ah! The devil has partitioned the Church and we are not even aware of it. The irony of it is that our followers are seeing all these anomalies. Could that not be the reason our followers are shouting *'to your tent o Israel,'* behind us (2 Sam. 20:1). Could it not be the reason many under-shepherds, many young Pastors, even those who are half-baked are clamouring for their own tents? *'It is the reason they are seeing visions of being call to start a work for the Lord elsewhere.'* How correct Jesus Christ was, hear what he said in one of His teachings –

> **"The disciple is not above his master: but every one that is perfect shall be as his master."** (Mk. 6:40)

We need to go back to the basics, let's see how the early Apostles were doing it, that makes the people to trust them so much as to go and be selling their properties and bringing it to the *'feet of the Apostles'.* Members who decide to offer strange fire amongst them received the same judgment as Nadab and Abihu, to proof that He is still the same God (Lev. 10:1-2; Acts 5:1-10). I think the challenge we have in the Church today is the fact that we are lazy, we cannot prayerfully sit with the scriptures to see beyond those who seemed to be our leaders. We are just swallowing everything presented to us hook, line, and sinker. Some of our leaders who got it right at the onset are now being carried away with different kinds of wave of doctrines. Methodology, strategies and trainings are replacing communion with the Holy Ghost and we are celebrating. Does it baffle you that people are not bringing their resources to the *'feet of the Apostles'* again? The truth of the matter is that most members know your secrets and they see you as a business man, selfish and greedy. It is high time you changed sir, so you do not become another Jeroboam the son of Nebat, who laid such bad precedence that no matter how terrible a king was in Israel, Jeroboam the son of Nebat was the measuring standard. God have mercy.

Like I said before, offering is much preferred to tithes, since the people were bringing everything they had, in the early Church, there was no need to ask them to bring tithe. The reason the Church revert to tithe was that the people were not giving offerings as it was done in the early Church. Offerings are to be given and received according to the needs of the body of Christ. That was what the Apostles saw with Jesus Christ, He only took offerings when the need arose, that we shall see in the next chapter.

CHAPTER 6

The Example of Jesus Christ on this Issue

Yes, like I said before, the Lord Jesus Christ took offerings from the people He ministered to.

Even from the point of His pregnancy, when the announcement was made to Mary she agreed to the proposal, to me that was an offering of oneself to the service of the Almighty God and humanity, she could have said no, but she willingly agreed - Lk. 1:26 – 38, remember offering must be given freely; that is the reason sometimes it is referred to as a freewill offering.

> *"Speak unto Aaron, and to his sons, and unto all the children of Israel, and say unto them, Whatsoever he be of the house of Israel, or of the strangers in Israel, that will offer his oblation for all his vows, and for all his <u>freewill offerings</u>, which they will offer unto the LORD for a burnt offering; Ye shall offer at <u>your own will</u> a male without blemish, of the beeves, of the sheep, or of the goats."* Lev. 22:18-19

In the book of Mat. 14:15-18. The Master had over 5, 000 people to feed at His crusade and when He made enquiry, He was told that, what was available in that desert was five loaves of bread and two small fishes, and according to John chapter 6:5-13, it was a little boy that made the supply. Looking at it with today's eyes. I will submit that, that boy was hawking at the crusade for his mother. In my own opinion that was an offering given by the boy and received by the Lord. May the Lord find pleasure in your offerings.

Likewise in Matthew chapter 15:32 - 38, over four thousand people were gathered with Him at another crusade ground where He ministered and He needed to feed them again. On this occasion, though we were not told who gave the offering (the seven loaves of bread), but sure enough, we were told that the Lord received and blessed it. May the blessings of the Lord be upon your offerings in the name of Jesus Christ.

From the above two examples, we got the wisdom that the quantity of the offering is not of any challenge to the Master, it is the quality that matters and the fact that it was what the Lord needed at that particular time makes it of enough quantity. Since it was to meet the need of the Lord, it also met the condition of whether it was commanded or not. The Lord who places a demand on that little offering in your hands knows what to do with it to meet the need at His hand; not only that, whenever God is demanding that which you have, remember that He was the One who gave it to you in the first place, which is the reason He may never complain about the quantity. There are many people in the Church who had kept back that which the Lord has been demanding from them, thinking it was too small an offering to give to the Lord. That is not a correct posture, what the word of God said was that each person must give according to their ability – Lev. 27:8; Ezr. 2:69; Acts 11:29; 1 Pet. 4:11. The man who refused to trade with his one talent was rebuked for his action – Mat. 25:24-28.

Now may we try to correct an error here, let's see this scripture together –

> *"Remember this—a farmer who plants only a few seeds will get a small crop. But the one who plants generously will get a generous crop ..."* (2 Cor. 6, NLT); *"Be not deceived; God is not mocked: for whatsoever a man soweth, that shall he also reap."* (Gal.6:7)

Some members of the body of Christ may quote these scriptures to their confusion. Even Pastors quote it to display their ignorance and or greed. They conclude that by these scriptures God wants you to give something big. Well, that truth has to be explained with the mind of the author. So, the question is who or what defines what you have as big or small? It is the God who gave to everyone as He so desire that may determine the size of what you brought as small or big. Take for example: *'When God called for offerings, Brother James who had a million naira in his possession gave a hundred thousand naira. Meanwhile Brother John who had five thousand naira in his possession gave five thousand. As far as man is concerned, Brother James gave more than Brother John, but as far as God is concerned Brother John gave more. Because he gave 100% of what he had in his possession'* -

> *"And Jesus sat over against the treasury, and beheld how the people cast money into the treasury: and many that were rich cast in much. And there came*

a certain poor widow, and she threw in two mites, which make a farthing. And he called unto him his disciples, and saith unto them, Verily I say unto you, That this poor widow hath cast more in, than all they which have cast into the treasury: For all they did cast in of their abundance; but she of her want did cast in all that she had, even all her living." Mk. 12:41-44

Another lesson from those guys who gave what they had to the Master to meet His needs is that, though God is the giver of all things, what He gave to one he may make it seed or meat. Seed is that one you gave as offering and meat is the one you consumed. The seed is the one that brings harvest, the meat is used to maintain your body and that is the end of it, it leaves your body to the toilet.

"For God is the one who provides seed for the farmer and then bread to eat. In the same way, He will provide and increase your resources and then produce a great harvest of generosity in you." 2 Cor. 9:10, so you may decide what to do with what God has given you.

I know you will agree with me that in Mat. 21:1 - 7, it was someone that owned the Ass the Master used for His triumphal entry into Jerusalem that day. To me that was an offering given by a man and received by the Lord. May your offerings be available when the Master is in need of them.

Also in the book of Lk. 5:1 - 3, He needed a platform to minister to the people that gathered to hear Him by the lake of Gennezareth, it was Peter that offered Him his boat to meet that need. That was also a giving and a receiving of an offering.

In preparation for His burial, He needed precious ointment for His body, which was supplied by a woman in the house of Simon the leper. That was a giving and receiving of offering – Mk. 14:3

Even at his burial, it was an offering from Joseph of Arimathaea that served as His tomb - Mat. 27:59 - 60.

These are just to mention a few, several individuals offered him lunch and dinner on different occasions and He was delighted in, and honoured their invitations. May the Lord honour our invitation in the name of Jesus Christ.

The common denominator in all of these instances was that He had a need and when the people around him offered what they had, He received them no matter how small, though in most of the cases, what they gave was multiplied and the giver went back with more than they came with. I assumed that the leftovers at those crusades were taking home by those who gave the little they had.

In my understanding therefore, I believe if any man gave anything to God as commanded, willingly and cheerfully in the service to the Lord, he must be handsomely rewarded, though this must not be the goal for offering things to the Lord. It must basically be based on the love for the King and His kingdom.

Before leaving this chapter, I think we should consider the position of the Master on tithe. Did He say anything about it? Did He approved or disapproved it? When He had the opportunity to talk about it, this is what He said -

"What sorrow awaits you teachers of religious law and you Pharisees. Hypocrites! For you are careful to tithe even the tiniest income from your herb gardens, but you ignore the more important aspects of the law – justice, mercy, and faith. You should tithe, yes, but do not neglect the more important things." (Mat. 23:23, NLT).

I have heard many believers say that Jesus Christ has come and has fulfilled the demands of the law on humanity. That is true, but remember as we have said before, tithe has been instituted before the law and the law that came several hundreds of years after did not abolish it – Gal. 3:17.

Just for emphasis, I like to repeat here again, that offerings preceded tithes and I think it is also preferred. The first set of people that gave offerings were Cain and Abel - Gen. 4:3-7. But with this record, it showed that it is not really our offerings that God desired, but our persons. When a man/woman is not accepted to God, his offerings are useless. He loves a cheerful giver who had first given himself on the altar of salvation.

CHAPTER 7

The Assemblywhere Members are not Faithful Tithers

The truth about tithes and offerings is that both of them are actually offerings. Tithes are limited to a tenth part of your earnings, incomes, profits, possessions and gifts. Most times tithes are periodic, but offerings are to be given as the occasion (God) demands.

We have discussed the reason for which God instituted offerings and tithes, therefore if a member or members of a particular assembly decides for whatever reason not to give their tithes and or offerings, the implication is what we are looking at here.

In the body of Christ, all have their roles to play, that is why it is called 'body' – 1 Cor. 12:12-31, all may not be Pastors, some have to be working on the altar, while others will be involved in secular business. Those working on the altar and those involved in secular businesses are all working for the same Lord and Master. But the arrangement is that, those involved in secular businesses should pay the bills of the members working on the altar so they will not have divided attention. Where do you think the government of nations got their civil service constitution that stipulates punishment for workers who are found doing something else outside of their official duties to make money? This was put in place to avoid divided attention.

I have said it in our discussions before this chapter, that tithes and offerings will never be a determining factor in your making heaven or not making heaven. Though I have read the testimonies of several people (who passed out and God mercifully returned them) on what our offerings and tithes may be used for when we eventually get to heaven, but no one has ever testified that he/she made heaven or they saw certain people in heaven because they were faithful tithers. Though the Lord Jesus Christ in the parable of the rich man and Lazarus (Lk. 16:19-31), singled out the fact that the rich man was not generous towards Lazarus as his undoing, but I tell you that he sure had several other ungodly behaviours that we were not told. The truth however is that when a man is neck deep in a particular sin, he is most likely to be involved with other sins. Mr. Sin rarely lives alone in any man's life, because that will easily lead to its extinction.

A person who is not born again and attends Church programmes and gives offering and tithes is like a man who takes money to a bank where he never had an account. At best his money may only be bundle-counted and kept somewhere until he does the needful - you may read the story of Cornelius for a better understanding on this (Act 10). The first thing a man required to be acceptable before the Lord is to become a member of the kingdom before thinking of giving offerings or tithes to God.

There are several instances when unbelievers were used in God's work, but ultimately it will serve them no use when they die. God does that when He has work that must be done and His children are not available. The case of kings like Artaxerxes in the time of Nehemiah (Neh. 2:2), Cyrus in the book of Isaiah 45:1; even Nebuchadnezzar was used to lift up Daniel in his kingdom, the Lord even called him his servant – Jer. 25:9. This is one of the reasons I said that those of you who are leaders in the body of Christ shouldn't be bothered about financing God's projects, God can raise anybody to achieve his purpose. He promised to raise children from the stones if His own people will not be available to do His work – Lk. 3:8.

When God gives you an assignment to be carried out for Him, He has a pattern. You will remember (if you are a Bible student), that God continuously emphasized to Moses while he was yet on the mountain that, he must do everything according to the pattern showed him on the mount – Exo. 25:40. God knows that people who may be brought to help you in the work will have their own ideas about how the work ought to be done. It is the duty of the visioner to always go back to the blue print of his meeting with the Lord to make sure that the pattern given to him is maintained. Aaron had an idea of the *gods* who led them out of Egypt – Exo. 32:1-4, Joshua had an idea of what was happening in the camp – Exo. 32:17; Num. 11:25-30, Peter had an idea of what should happen to the Lord – Mat. 16:22-23, and John too also had an idea of who ought to use the name of their Master – Lk. 9:49-50. That is why it is dangerous to start a work for the Lord when He has not commanded it. What is going to be the pattern? At best, you will be a carbon-copy. You must let the people that God is bringing into the work with you know that, this was not even your own idea. They must know that you may never add to it or remove from it – Jos. 1:8; 2 Cor. 11:3-4. As a leader, you must make the vision plain to your followers until they have understood every bit of it. Once that happened, they will be good to go, and their commitment will be total. That was what happened in the early Church. You need not worry that some are leaving because of your adherence to what the Lord gave you. The One who gave you the work to do must remain at the center of it all. The Lord Jesus Christ never begged anyone to stay with His vision, and no one was cajoled, not even the rich young ruler – Mk. 10:17-25. Most times, those who see themselves as financiers may want to have their inputs into the work and when you insist, they may hold on to their resources – *you see, it was their resources,* it was never God's, that is why you don't need it. And in the event that it was kept in their care to support the work initially (it is possible that God has spoken to you about them before they came), Sir, even then you don't need to worry, they are the losers. God have alternatives that are better. The major challenge of such individuals is that they have not grown enough to know that what they had does not belong to them. It is the reason that you as the one that God called must raise and train those God are bringing to you. Make sure they know the Lord properly, they must be genuinely born again and followed up to mature before they are accepted to even give to the Lord, else they will soon become the black sheep. When your followers are well rooted in the word of life and in the things of God, they will willingly give themselves to the work.

There are people worshiping in an assembly and they don't give their tithes there for whatever reason(s), lack of scriptural understanding is at the foundation of such attitude. This is the word of the Lord about tithe –

> *"Bring ye all the tithes into the <u>storehouse</u>, that there may be meat in mine house ..."*

by the *'storehouse'*, it indicates that that is where you are getting nourished. The man of God who labours over your life to feed and to pray for you is entitled to your tithe and not anyone else, he is commanded to feed from that storehouse. What you are allowed to do to other men of God or other assemblies is at best to give them offerings and that must also be commanded, otherwise it must be done where you are worshiping. I have said it before, your tithe is what God has given to the priest who serves on the altar as his inheritance – Num. 18:21. I see many people saying that their Pastors or leaders are getting fat, feasting on their tithes, but isn't that what God has given to them to feed on? God never commanded you as a member of His body to help Him monitor how the tithe is spent or maybe I have not discovered it. This is very important. It is an act of insubordination, for members to be questioning how their Pastors/leaders spent their tithes. The fact that people are doing it all over the places does not give it a divine backing. The scripture says you should not follow multitudes to do evil – Exo. 23:2. Well, if it is the law of the land that says that the finance of the Church should be audited, that may be okay, but even then, the government ought to know that men of God are not answerable to them, because they were not the ones who gave them the work to do, and *'if you did not give me an assignment, you should not expect me to submit my work to you'*. The truth however, is that the people in government who are unbelievers have no fault in this, some of them feared God more than the people in the Church. Some of the people in the Church who are close to the top in the Churches and in the government quarters are the ones stirring evil and sponsoring animosities against the Church. That is unfortunate, but it points to the fact, Sanballat, Tobiah (Neh. 4:1-7), Tatnai – Ezr. 5, and the likes of Judas are still here with us – Mat. 26:14-16. People who will for the love of money sell their leaders. These are the people who watches from the back only to pick on the weaknesses and the fault of their leaders. Some of them even pretend to be family friends of their leaders, so as to be so close enough to get all the information they need to pull the carpet under their leaders; what an evil generation! There are some of them also, who would have been working secretly amongst the brethren campaigning against the happenings and the progress of the Church, but when they think it is not working properly, they will use the influence they have in the government, and once the law is enacted, even when they are long gone the *'odour of their waste'* will still be around. Some of them do so because they are jealous of the man of God. Some do so because they wanted certain positions and privileges and it was not given to them because the Lord has not commanded it. Some of them will never remember that when these men of God were going about, doing all they could to make sure the work of God on their hands prospered and is established, they had gone through hell several times over, in the cold and in the sun. It is the reason such individuals can never go far. It is not impossible for you to see some anomaly in the system, your duty is to go to the Lord in the place of prayer, so you may know what to do about it instead of going about to run your mouth. If you are so sure that God has ordained you to be part of the work in that assembly, then leaving will also not help you. And in the event that God is asking you to leave, do so in peace.

What a man is losing when he is not supporting the work of God that he is called to support is much, the danger can only be left to imagination. As you give your offerings in your place of worship, you are helping God to pay His bills and as such make Him a shareholder in your businesses. And by now you should have known that God will never play the second fiddle wherever He is, it then means that He becomes the chairman of your business and when God is the chairman of your business you know what that means. It is impossible for that business to fail. How will God allow a business from where His bills are being paid to go down or go bankrupt? I have noticed that one of the reasons, employees give their best to their employers is that they know that if the company goes down, they will lose their income. If men will do this, how much more God.

When you as a member of an assembly refuse to pay your tithes and give your offerings, you put your Pastors/leaders on the edge. How? You may want to ask? And I say that these may happen in several ways. God's intention for the priests is to do nothing else apart from the service in the tabernacle and on the altar. When you refuse to honour this ordinance, you cause them to be distracted, they may become deceptive, frustrated and at the extreme of it they may abandon the work. It is the reason men o f God host programmes God never commanded – seven super Sundays with outrageous captions, organizing special breakthrough services, special seven days of powerful prayers, multimillionaire crusades, special evangelical outreaches to bring more members to the Church, special offerings and launchings, selling of special holy water and anointing oil, etc. When men of God are involved in these things and many more to make money, it is because members are not faithfully committed to the ordinance of tithes and offerings. Many have even gone as far as consulting media and using diabolical means, those of them that are more technical on this are faking miracles, to draw men to their assemblies. The danger in this is that when such *'men of God'* had already made money through such programmes, the probability that they will stop is not there, because they think that stopping means that the cash flow will cease. Members of the Church who are not faithful in these ordinances (tithe and offering) are the reason many real men of God have left their duty posts to go and be looking for that which was never lost in the first place. Brethren, never forget that these men of God have obligations as you have. They have wives and children, some of them have more dependants than you know, it is even worse than ever now, when everybody seemed to believe that all Pastors are rich. So, when they are not giving to people as they expected, they concluded that such Pastors are stingy and selfish.

Please note, this exposition is not aimed to make members become sympathetic, no it is to let you understand your duty as members of your assembly, it is also not aimed at boosting the priests' ego. We all have our part to play in this, so that the devil may be silenced on this and kept where he belonged, and that the kingdom may advance as the Master desired it. Ignorance about God's plan for us is terrible – Hos. 4:6. This scripture revealed that they were God's people but as long as they were ignorant of God's provision for them, the enemy took advantage of them. Consider the grace upon Apostle Paul: I never read that he took tithe, though there were occasions when he took offerings, which wasn't that he asked for it, the Philippian brethren just have the understanding that this is something they must do, and the Apostle was glad they did. Because he will not ask for offering and tithe, he had to be working as a tent maker to support himself – Acts 18:1-3; 20:33-35. He was not supposed to be working to support himself, according to his own teaching, which am sure he was led to teach by the Holy Ghost.

You may please read Phil. 4: 10-19. He had earlier taught, writing to the Corinthian and Galatian brethren that those who are working on the altar ought to partake with the altar. He said those who are taught in the word should provide for their teachers in all good things – 1 Cor. 9:1-15; Gal. 6:6. He said that he did not enforce this principle because he would not allow anyone to glory over him, but that is not what the scripture commanded us to do. Just like He said in that 1 Cor. 9:7, the man who planted a vineyard ought to eat of the fruit. Where the people are willing to give and the man of God is not receiving, the man of God is obstructing the flow of the people's blessing.

Let's conclude this discussion by saying that it is a privilege to be a blessing to God's work, so those of you who are contemplating withdrawing your support for the work of God or have done so already, do so to your own disadvantage. God will never beg any man to support His work, but as a man who receives grace to admonish you at a time like this, go and sit with this, pray about it and put on your faith cap. Let go of all that you are thinking and let God. You will be glad you did.

CHAPTER 8

Final Admonition

According to the grace given to me, I like you to part with this. God does not need any of us to achieve His goals, yet He needs you to achieve His goals. I hope this does not sound confusing? Or does it?

God is all sufficient, that is why He is called El-shadai. However, He has committed the earth to the hands of men – Psa. 115:16, in essence, it is men that He will use to achieve His goals here on the earth. It then means that if you will not release yourself and resources to God for the kingdom use, He will use another man, since He owns everyone including non-Christians. To proof to us that He will get His things done no matter what, there are occasions when He has either come down Himself or sent His angels to achieve certain goals (Judg. 13:1-20; Lk. 1:5-17), but definitely if He find a man who can be used to achieve it, He prefers that to any other alternative, especially the one who is willing and upright in his ways - 1 Chro. 29:17; Jhn. 6:38.

This is to the men of God serving in the New Testament Church. I have heard many teachings from reputable sons of God, that only born again, heaven bound believers may give acceptable offerings to God. This also is not a complete truth. The Lord God Almighty took offering from several individuals that were not seen as His people and that we have discussed in the last chapter. The Lord Jesus Christ Himself received offerings from people who were not his followers. For example, Peter was not yet a disciple when the Master used his ship to minister – Lk. 5:1-3. The animal He used for His triumphal entry into Jerusalem probably belonged to someone who is not His disciple – Mat. 21:1-3. He accepted invitation to dine with the Pharisees – Lk. 7:36; 11:37. The woman who anointed the feet of the Lord with her tears and oil was considered a sinner, yet the Lord accepted her offering – Lk. 7:36-38. Even in our age I have heard testimonies of how the Lord used unknown persons to solve certain problems for `His servants. I have also heard the testimonies from men of God who refused to take offerings sent to them through some people and they suffered the consequence. What must be done therefore is to first confirm with God, to be sure that He was the One who sent them to you. After all, it is not all offerings given by believers that are acceptable to God. Eliab and other six sons of Jesse was presented to God and He rejected them – 1 Sam. 16:8-10. David the very Ideal king of Israel offered to build the LORD a temple and God refused him – 1 Chro. 22:7-8. When you refuse the offerings sent to you, you will suffer unnecessarily. If it is only you that will suffer, it may be okay, but you will also block the blessings meant for such individual's obedience. Do not assume that they may be blessed even when their offerings are not accepted by you. Only seeds that are sown may bring harvest. More importantly is that seeds sown in the correctly prescribed soil are sure of rewards.

To you members of the body of Christ, know this as you come to this faith, you belong to God – 1 Cor. 6:19-20. There is nothing you have that has not been given to you – 1 Cor. 4:7. You will be wise then to give Him access to all that you are including your wealth. Please note and this is very important just for emphasis God gives to every one of us as He so desire, what He gave to you is not the limit of what He has – Mat. 25:15.

But what God has given to one, he/she may make seed out of it (tithes and offerings), and another may make everything he/she received bread (food) – Isa. 55:10. Never forget this, it is the seed you sowed that may bring you harvest, the one you made bread is used to maintained your body and the larger part of it goes to the toilet, depending on your age.

Finally, I like to say that tithe is not about your Pastor or your church it is about God, you and your future.

www.ingramcontent.com/pod-product-compliance
Lightning Source LLC
Chambersburg PA
CBHW060352130626
46553CB00003B/1197